Living Lockdown

Preben Andersen

O&U
Onwards & Upwards

Onwards and Upwards Publishers

4 The Old Smithy
London Road
Rockbeare
EX5 2EA
United Kingdom

www.onwardsandupwards.org

First edition, published in the United Kingdom by Onwards and Upwards Publishers Ltd. (2021).

ISBN: 978-1-78815-582-3
Typeface: Sabon LT

About the Author

 I was born in Aarhus, Denmark on November 20th, 1950 but have been living permanently in Britain since 1975. I married Margaret in 1977 and we have three children, six grandchildren, two step-grandchildren and one step-great-great-grandchild (at the last count!)

Having started my working life in Britain working in administration for a Danish marine paints company for 18 years, I felt the call to enter the Methodist ministry, from which I retired at the end of July 2020. Margaret and I now live happily in Clevedon, North Somerset, and in retirement it is my fervent wish to continue my love for writing.

Over the years I have tried my hand at most genres, including three little books with my beloved, now departed collie springer Zoe (I was the woof-reader). I also wrote a short poetry collection, *Travellers All*. Both the Zoe books and the poetry were published privately, but only in a few hundred copies and with the profits going to church charitable purposes. My collection of poems and the reflections you are now about to read are my first attempts at possibly becoming known to a wider readership…

I should perhaps also mention that over the years I have written regular columns entitled *Thought for the Weak* to the secular press. A book of the same name containing a collection of the best of these columns is due to be published soon by Onwards and Upwards Publishers.

Living Through Lockdown starts with the news of the pandemic and finishes with the welcome news of the first of many vaccines about to be rolled out, as modern parlance goes. I should perhaps have carried on and waited to see how the vaccination programme works out, but I decided that this is as good a place to stop as any, with good and welcome news and yet with every reason not to rush but continue to be careful and prayerful as we face a new and surely happy year, 2021.

Each poem and reflection has a date. My readers may remember and recall their own feelings and emotions on the dates I refer to. I am sure there is much left out and many important aspects of the year I have perhaps forgotten – or chosen to ignore? I don't know.

It is my prayer and my hope that my readers will find something in this collection to stimulate, encourage, bring a smile, or perhaps a tear; in fact, any or all of those, and if there is anything you would like to share with me, please do not hesitate to contact me at any time on my e-mail address:

pwandersen@btinternet.com

Every blessing,

Preben
December 2020

Endorsements

The 'Great Dane' uses his adopted second language to bless us with an array of words to get us through these pandemic days. Preben's boyish enthusiasm shines through each reflection, story and poem, and his deep care for God's world pours out of the pages. Reverend Andersen hits that rare mark between thoughtfulness and humour. A blessing in these strange times.

Rev. Gordon Gresswell

If you have been in the Forces, the expression 'Sky-pilot' will be familiar. Preben Andersen was the Chaplain to the Caldicot Branch of the Royal British Legion and came to us as the first Methodist, and the first Dane, to hold the role. He became a great friend of all and always had time for any who needed a shoulder. His talks on Remembrance Day, often aimed at the children, were a star-turn. Tall, quietly spoken and humble, his poetry, writing and enthusiasm for people hugely impressed me, even after a lifetime of cynicism towards religion. A 'Sky-pilot' of the very best.

Gordon Hill
President, Caldicot & District Branch
The Royal British Legion

Contents

Preface

This is a fresh collection of poems and reflections from someone rekindling his roots after having tried many other forms of expressing his love for words, sometimes successfully, sometimes not. This collection starts with us all in the throes of the coronavirus pandemic but I pray that by the time it finishes we'll be well out of it and rid of it for good!

Alongside my poems I have also, in the early stages of the pandemic and up until my retirement, provided regular bulletins and short videos for church websites, but that is another story...

I dedicate this collection to my beloved wife Margaret who so inspired me today in her 'Coffee with God' Bible study (where we shared our views on miracles) that I went straight home and started writing this.[1]

Talking about miracles, here is a memory that has now kickstarted it all once more and which I shared briefly with the group today. Not a poem, and yet I believe with a poetic streak to it that I hope to find again in what I write.

Thought for the Weak

Published in a Barnstable Newspaper, 25.03.1999

It was something so normal that many people would not even think to stop and look. Something so absurd to most, I guess, that even writing about it will seem a waste of time to

---

[1] Written on 12 March 2020

some. And yet, to me it had such an impact that I have not been able to wrestle it from my mind.

It happened when I took Old Sheba to the Burrows for her lunchtime constitutional about a week ago. There, in the middle of the pebbles and rocks by the dried-up river sat a single daffodil, enclosed, squashed almost, by two fairly big pieces of rock and yet managing to peep through in splendid colour and with the stem obviously having found the smallest bit of moist grass or sand amidst all the rock.

I looked around to see if there were other daffodils on the Burrows and found to my relief that this was indeed the only one as far as the eye could see. I wanted it so much to be unique and it was! Better still, I have no doubt that when I go there tomorrow, my flower in all its pride and splendid isolation will stand just as tall as ever as a symbol of spring, of Easter just around the corner!

I like the story of the young lad who came home from Sunday School on Easter Sunday and told his mother he could understand about Jesus well enough, but he was not too clear about the roses! So he asked his mum, "Why was Jesus a rose?" Christ a rose indeed! He did arise, or rather he was risen – just like my daffodil has arisen where you would least expect it to, on rocky ground, with little fertile soil, yet more than enough to keep it fresh and beautiful and alive. Here is hope in all its majesty and glory, even through the miracle of a modest flower. Amazing how the simple things in nature, in life, can trigger something very profound.

One of my favourite choruses starts, "Open our eyes, Lord, we want to see Jesus." Well, something as trivial, as everyday, as a constitutional with my dog certainly opened my eyes! That day I saw Jesus there in the midst of God's humblest creation...

How Could I Ever Doubt?

How could I ever doubt, Lord, this is where I should be
Stringing words together in Christian harmony
Looking unto Thee, Lord, for inspiration, grace
To wander in Thy footstep and reach that glorious place
Where awesome truths emerge and I find a word of Thine
That I can take and personalize to make entirely mine.
It started with a poem so many years ago
But rather than continue and let the spirit flow
I turned to other writings, some helpful, many dire,
And looking back, quite failing to strengthen and inspire.
So back it is to poetry, I ask my God to find
The means to search the beaten track with a courageous
  mind
Emptied of all but love for Him who tread my path before
The One with whom I now attempt my journey to restore.

12.03.2020

Coronavirus UK

Between 5-10,000 people expected to carry the virus at its peak.

Out of a population of 60 million.

Media fever gripping the nation, one dares hardly sniffle or cough…

Self-isolate, self-isolate is the command.

(A bit like Doctor Who, really – exterminate, exterminate.)

Do we listen to the advice or do we think it's never me, always someone else?

Holidays cancelled or at best postponed. Indefinitely.

Flights interrupted in their thousands. You may get out but no guarantee you'll get back. And if you're lucky you'll be quarantined. Or die if you're unlucky.

Countries shutting down completely.

Cruises banned, handshakes too.

Big gatherings curtailed. Industry shaking. Financial markets exploding. And imploding. Total collapse. Into nothingness.

Travel restricted, special permission required, offenders fined and sometimes jailed, doubts arising, tempers flaring, and soon the shout goes out: Enough is enough. Time to move on. We are impatient people.

Virus peaking and levelling out? We don't know yet. Only God knows. But God does know. Do we understand and accept what God knows? Dare we trust ourselves in His hands? Is there anything else we can or should be doing, ourselves, with Him, or without?

God knows!

12.03.2020

This is Your Virus Speaking

Oh dear, worried now, eh?

Thinking perhaps that this is the planet as we know it coming to an end?

Yet at the same time suddenly seeing the atmosphere improving. The stratosphere even. Cleaner air. Less pollution. Being able to breathe again. If only you were allowed to be outside and enjoy it. Which you aren't.

Trying to get rid of me? Yes, of course you are. I accept that. And you will. One day. Someone will get to the bottom of me. And quite right too.

I do not want to see so many suffer. But one day the planet said, enough is enough, and looked to me to do something about it all. And I am. Doing something about it all.

And it takes a long time. And it's hard. And it breaks your heart. And mine.

Am I enjoying this? No. Am I almost finished? Sadly, no. Are we talking months? Yes. Years? Maybe. If not of me then of some other virus, no doubt – unless of course the planet says, at long last they are beginning to listen. To see sense.

Is God in all this? I am sure He is. If only from a distance at the moment. Seeing how you, his people, react first. He gave you all free will, after all. To do what is right and even to rectify all that is bad. To him it is never too late to turn back and start afresh.

Is there evil in this? And am I evil? No. And no. If it hadn't been me being chosen, the planet would have chosen some other form of messenger. And it may still when I am dead and gone; if nothing has been learned while I am still on the warpath... But it's nothing to do with evil. It has all to do with common sense.

So wake up, people. Everywhere. Continue to search for something somewhere to see me off. Turn back to God and his ways. And do it soon. Pray. Pray that this may all come to an end soon. Say the Lord's Prayer in whatever language. As someone has already suggested, say the Lord's Prayer as you wash your hands, or Psalm 23, or both, instead of singing Happy Birthday.

Who wants to sing Happy Birthday anyway, right now? I know many who say they are putting their birthdays on hold. For what is the point? We can't celebrate without a party. And we mustn't party.

So, friends, keep trusting, keep searching for a cure. Get rid of me, please, for I am not enjoying this any more than you are. A lot less in fact. For I am dying but you may still have the chance of something far better and longer lasting than you ever imagined in God's hands. In a cleaner environment with so much more love and care and understanding. As soon as I am here no longer. And why not start now? Goodbye friends, and God bless you as in time and hopefully soon I prepare to take my leave and you prepare to look and listen to the planet who is God's and dying to be revived and revigorated once again by you who are her custodians with God by your side.

19.03.2020

Feeling Okay

A poem purposely written in a very irregular rhythm.

Feeling okay, today – sort of, at least – though with a beast of a dull ache of ear (and tooth to boot) that I cannot refute and which goes to the root of my threshold of pain but I will not be slain, so battling on...

My beloved is well or, if she is not, she will not tell and I daren't ask too many a time as it would be a crime to think I am fussing and have her cussing my unwanted worry so here in a hurry: she too battles on...

We manage a walk and a smile and a talk but cannot hold hand, it's a desolate land, as with some distance between and wearing our glove we walk through the park, avoiding the masses, all hiding their love...

But hiding it only by outward appearance, escaping the clearance and quick disappearance of families talking and dog walkers walking their pets on a lead, on a mission, no lingering, must get back at full speed.

With much worse to come and sheer agony for some it's a doomsday disaster that moves ever faster across the wide length of the Channel at strength, with no lack in speed; will the virus succeed in making these Isles the focus of trials that others have suffered with no mercy offered?

Yes, feeling okay, but how long until our vision of hope turns – against our will – to deaths on our streets we could never foresee as we ask ourselves:

Could it be even me?

22.03.2020

Battling On

Unlike many sadly already perished we carry on well
My wife and I
While heads of state and princes too go through their hell
The question why:
Not us, the meek, the low, the poor, the often barely seen
But those of fame
Who govern, reign with images in papers and on screen
The famous name

Is it to say that this corona differs not between the lowly and
the high?
Is it to show that all precautions being equal, some will die?
Is it perhaps a warning to us all against complacency?
Is it a way to make us ask and wonder who the next might
be?

And meanwhile we battle on
It's all we can do
By the darkness of the moon and the rising of the sun
We hope to see this through

In the turmoil of our mind
In the peace God helps us find
In the hope of restoration
For this and future generation
We battle on, we battle on
We battle on...

28.03.2020

Hair Today, Gone Tomorrow

How long before we shall all walk round with hairs and beards not unlike those of the cavemen of old?

"With not a barber in sight"
My wife said the other night
"Or a hairdresser open for me
I wonder how long it will be
Before we walk round in a haze
With our hairs preventing us gaze
On the world we so used to know
But now just can't see where might go."

Her words made me stop, made me think
And almost reduced me to drink
As only this morning when getting up
And shaving and washing I had to stop
When looking at me in that mirror at front
Was what best is described as a mastodont!

Unruly, unkempt and unwieldly indeed
I couldn't remain, left the bathroom at speed
While hunting for scissors and blades to reduce
The forest of hairs everywhere, but no use
The damage was done, point of no return
We're so quick to assume yet so slow to learn...

So now as we sit at the table with hairs
That threaten to cover the back of our chairs
We look to the day when from self-isolation
Our barbers and dressers see our exasperation

And welcome us back to put our heads in their hand
And take us once more to the promised land.

31.03.2020

4,000 Beds

In memory of Florence Nightingale (1820-1910). A reflection.

In East London.
Of all places.
The world's biggest hospital.
Ever.
Existing buildings converted in no time at all and now
    waiting to receive their first patients.
Those most seriously affected by coronavirus.
Some will die.
Many will be too ill to realize where they are about to enter.

The Nightingale hospital.
Our angels on earth, the nurses, waiting to welcome.
Receive.
Cure.
In the footsteps of Florence.
But some will be reduced to sit and hold a hand and pray
    and comfort those who will not live.
4000 beds.
So many will arrive.
And all will one day leave.
But not all on their own two feet.
Some must leave in boxes.

Florence.
Nightingale.
Not a building but a person.
The founder of modern nursing no less.
Served in the Crimean War.

Became known as the Lady with the Lamp for the rounds
she made of wounded soldiers at night.

Founded St Thomas' hospital in London.
1860.
The first secular nursing school in the world, now part of
King's College in London.
The highest international distinction a nurse can achieve, the
Florence Nightingale Medal, was named in her honour.
And she herself received awards: The Royal Red Cross, the
Lady of Grace of the Order of St John, and the Order of
Merit.

Nightingale.
A hospital.
4,000 beds.
Florence Nightingale.
One nurse.

Coronavirus.
A curse.
A pain.
For a while.
But not forever.

East London.
A place.
Waiting to welcome those desperately ill.
Doors opening tomorrow.
People, nurses, working, loving, caring in the footstep of
Florence.
Florence Nightingale.

Virus.
What virus?
You are already beaten.

31.03.2020

Resurrection Power 2020

Easter thoughts following a graveside service in a country church-yard.

From the ashes a new beginning, with glory, in hope
An assurance that in and through it all, we'll cope
A smile least expected but met and responded to in love
Our trust in each other confirmed – and in Him above
Even with just a few in a churchyard so bleak and bare
Committing to the ground a loving soul so full of care
Who spent her life fostering hundreds of girls and boys
Teaching them values and morals, and heavenly joys
Saying farewell to a loved one – restrictions in place –
Keeping the distance, like robbers, a mask to cover the face
Yet – in togetherness, sun shining bright – and dwelling in
     peace
Taking the time to remember and smile, to cry, be at ease
And soon to return when all this has been and gone
To sit by the grave at the tree on the bench – the beloved
     one
So far yet so near, always dear, always here
Apart for a while but still sharing the smile
That opened up lives for so many a child
Through faith and good morals delivered in mild
Loving gestures of caring and daring for me
To become the best person in life I could be!

Herein lies the power, the spirit's endurance
To show His good works in the gift of assurance
That the great gift of Easter with all it entails

Is all down to God from whom Power hails
We praise Him this Easter for helping us know
That *He* is eternal wherever *we* go…

09.04.2020

Indomitable Spirits

Boris bouncing back.

Captain Tom celebrating his 100th birthday having raised hundreds of thousands for NHS, walking step by step, for weeks on end, with the help of his Zimmer...

Boris recuperating at Chequers.

Italy and Spain beginning to relax lockdown measures. China reporting more than a hundred new cases after weeks of none at all. May this be a warning against complacency and a call to stand firm.

Boris preparing to take charge yet again but must be patient.

Parliament planning to reconvene a week from now, but how? Meetings about relaxing some of our measures, but when? And for whom? Talks about a gradual return to work for the few but not the many. Who will choose and who are the chosen?

Boris battling his impatience to gather new strength. To lead from the front yet again.

Opposition getting ready to do what they do best. Oppose. Yet promising to compromise wherever possible and come together. The public hoping and praying but still to be convinced. Mudslinging has started. Apportioning blame. Already. What could have gone better? What should have been done better? At whom can we point the finger?

Boris getting ready, knowing he is in charge, that ultimately the buck ends with him. But confident, assured. Recharged, renewed.

And finally, the rest of us. You and I. Watching. Doing what we are told. Well, most of us anyway, and most of the time at least. Trusting those in the know, supposedly. At the same time, all of us, fighting an unknown enemy so unlike any other we have ever come across.

Our indomitable spirits. They are what keep us going. Each one of us. Undying faith. Immortal love. The spiritual dimension in each one of us, often unseen, sometimes not felt, but always there. Undying compassion, total sacrifice, oh power of God.

Boris. We trust you. You trust us. But may we all put our trust in Him who gave His all. For us.

13.04.2020

Levelling Out?

Are things improving, have we reached the peak?
Still much more data to sift through and graphs to tweak.
What goes for one poor nation may not in fact apply
To other states and continents where still so many die
And where in fact the bug returns and strikes the people
    twice
There may still be some way to go before we dare to rise
And pray and hope from all our hearts the end may now be
    near
While asking God to keep us strong and take away our fear.

O save us from complacency in thinking all is well
When still for many thousands we are living through a hell
Of great uncertainty and loss and many lives on hold
While we each try to ascertain how all this might unfold

We pray for wisdom, guidance, faith and trust at every turn
We pray the resurrection hope in every heart may burn
As step by step we face the dangers open to us all
Beside the Shepherd – always there – to carry when we fall.
Levelling out? Maybe, maybe not. Still highs and lows ahead
So may we leave our worries here and look to Him instead.

13.04.2020

Nature's Might

In the garden birds are singing,
From empty church a bell still ringing?
In the trees the wind is moving,
Breathing gentle symphony.
In the street no cars are racing,
Empty shops and precincts facing
A new stillness, tender peace
To lift our spirits high and free.

All around us now we hear it,
Now we see it, now we feel it,
God's creation recreated in
The things we took for granted.
Everywhere as all is silenced,
All on hold yet re-emerging;
Can we see the newfound Eden,
God-created, freshly planted?

When all this is in the past,
We know it wasn't meant to last,
May nature's song still linger
In our mind and in our heart;
The peace we find so difficult
But there to help us see again
The beauty of the world we love
As once again we start.

And may that start be grounded
In God's first creative breath
When from a state of emptiness

He gave us life and death,
But more than that – eternal breath
To saviour His own peace
In that full and glorious majesty
He wants us to release.

13.04.2020

Terry Quinlan's Last Poem –
In Memoriam

Written on April 1st, 2020, as dictated to his wife Beryl.

God is speaking by His Spirit,
Speaking to a changing world.
Through His Son, our great Lord Jesus,
To His people, love unfurled.

Mystified by woes and fears
We turn to leaders for release.
Lift our eyes, Lord, from the earth
And see the Cross for Jesus' peace.

God bless you, Terry, one of John Wesley's great preachers and a true friend of mine.

Going Live?

While waiting to see if I have managed to transfer my first ever live video to my webmaster – and secretly hoping that I may have failed miserably!

Will it, won't it, don't know yet
But if it won't I shall not fret
For deep inside I know full well
The only story I can tell
Is print on my paper my thoughts to keep
While all this tech stuff makes me weep!
They want me though to have a go
At podcast – broadcast – video
So in the end I thought, ah well
If meant to be then time will tell
But as I write naught has come through
And secretly I mutter, 'Phew!'
In the vain hope that nothing will
But can't be really sure until
The day is gone and Roger says
I cannot sit here all my days
And try and fathom what you've done
My patience now is almost gone
That's when I know I'm good and clear
And have no reason now to fear
That I shall make it, so to speak
To join the technocratic league
For deep inside my soul I know
That as for me, one way to go
To wander the old-fashioned way

And gladly face another day
With quill and inkpot, paper too
Suffices me – how about you?

20.04.2020

Postscript 21.04.2020
My first ever personal video was posted on our church website this morning. Serves me right, I guess?

Boris Bouncing Back

Written on the day that Boris Johnson returned to 10, Downing Street, a lot thinner, somewhat quieter, but with the true bulldog spirit for us all to see and hear.

Boris bouncing back – no curtailing him now
Talking sense to the common man, taking a bow
Sensing the love in the air for his ways and manner
Taking it all in his stride while flying the banner
No empty promises here but plenty of zest
Reminding us all where we are and joining the quest
For more hopeful times, for normalization to come
Though normal won't be for the many but maybe for some?
For 'normal' has gone, nothing the same, the old ways must
    perish
While facing a future of longing for much we so used to
    cherish
While finding in newness of spirit and getting together
The means that enable each seeker our problems to weather
For all things are here for a reason and nothing in vain
And without the new birth in death and love grown from
    our pain
We cannot proceed and work through to the sunshine ahead
And look to the day when assurance replaces our dread.
So Boris, no pressure, we look to you doing your best
To speak the right words and again help us swim on a crest
Of laughter and praying, let nothing us overwhelm
Now that we have you back to strength firm and strong at
    the helm!

27.04.2020

Each Drumbeat a Heartbeat for the NHS

On the day our Richard's old drum set, stored for years upstairs in the church, finally found a new and even better home...

The rhythm of life for the NHS
   as someone will put together a set of drums
Long forgotten, long abandoned
   yet never disappeared
A donation to be given to help
   the life-blood flow and the fever stabilize
And someone somewhere return to health
   and a new beginning
An old set of drums gathering dust
   but no longer so as soon, very soon
When fitted together
   they will grace someone's home
With a new rhythm of pulsating love
   and kindness and vigour
Stamping out the virus as the sounds are merging
   and the backing provided
To all those other instruments
   forming the rhythm of life
In someone's home
   as much as in a concert hall
With just a few listening in
   rather than thousands
Each beat, each sound drowning out
   the sorrow, the sadness

The pain and the sheer desolation
   felt by so many
In lockdown in solitude,
   enforced isolation

As the beat of an old set of drums
Brought back to life
Sends money to those who help
Giving hope to so many
As the music goes on with our faith undiminished
Through the beat of a drum

29.04.2020

Come Monday

Come Monday…
Will some kind of normal return?
Will some be allowed back to work?
Will masks be a must for the many?
Will young people now be set free
While old people stay where they are?
Will free will be gone through the roof?
Restrictions afresh put in place?
Will apps now replace common sense?
Will smartphones control what we do?
Will all that we are and all that we hope to be
Be controlled by machines
By decreed interference
Leaving us numb
And with nowhere to go?
Come Monday…
Will some kind of normal return?

06.05.2020

Doctor Who

On receiving the news from Doctor Who (or the World Health Organization) that at least half a dozen further symptoms should be added to loss of smell, loss of taste, loss of breath, unusual cough and peculiar fever to determine whether you have coronavirus or not.

One does wonder when total loss of common sense might be included too...

So here we are, it's make or break
There can't be many roads to take
That will not help you diagnose
You suffer much from one of those!
A sneeze, a cough – but out of place
Some specialist right in your face
To warn you to self-isolate
Your own small corner to create...
Then out of nowhere, lo, behold
Some feverish shivers quite untold
Come barging in and lay you low
With not an inkling where to go
And just as soon as smell and taste
Start going, now you need make haste
As added to the other two
You race, resorting to the loo
Oh boy, that was the final straw
What next, I ask, can there be more?
How come it happens just to me
Can all this Covid-19 be?
Is it the virus by default?

Is there some way I can cry, "Halt!"
And ask to leave me well alone
Or has decorum been – and flown?
Is there no longer hope to find
In heart and prayer, trust and mind
That nothing surely is so bad
That there is nothing to be had
By way of antidote or cure
To help us all feel more secure?

And time goes on and tempers flare
Emotions, anger now laid bare
Until we ask in all this why
We do not just lie down and die?

19.05.2020

Zooming In

A prayer in preparation for a Caldicot stewards' meeting.

Let us pray.
Oh Lord, give us this day
Patience of heart and mind
In what we hope to say
And in our sharing find.
Give us a listening ear
And lips for honest talk
As through this time of fear
We take the Godly walk.
But above all, O Lord
We pray you will enable
And by your grace afford
A well-connected cable!
May Zoom see us at ease
As we our meeting start
And may the links not "freeze"
So we can all take part
With thanks for this technology
For without that where would we be?
Thank you, Lord. Amen.

21.05.2020

With Just a Few More Months to Go

Two months almost to the day
And we will be well on our way
About to stop the work we do
And venture into pastures new...
Ten years of ministry galore
Could I in truth have asked for more?
Have I achieved what I had hoped
Had there been more – would I have coped?
Are now with the decisions made
The right to slowly make things fade
More prominent in heart and mind
Or unasked questions still to find?
Did both of us do well enough?
Did we pull back when it got tough?
Did some small venture have its day?
Or stopped too soon? – it's hard to say.
Do we now go with peace of mind
To pastures new with people kind
Who will enable and permit
To let us settle in and knit
This brand-new pattern of our lives
Where toil may cease yet fortune strives
To help us see beginnings new
Of simply *be* – not have to *do*?
We now prepare in harmony
For what God knows is yet to be

With thanks for ten years in this place
As into Clevedon Hills we gaze...

31.05.2020

1984 Revisited?

George Orwell wrote the book that caused a riot
But after the commotion things went quiet
And life returned to some normality...
Now with this long pandemic at the fore
It seems we're losing patience ever more
As anger grows and all good morals flee.

Again the hatred shows itself alive
Despite the way that most of us still strive
To do the decent things in life and pray
That soon this evil virus yet unbeat
May soon be conquered and, please God, retreat
As we together seek a better way.

For hatred raises now its ugly head
And fills the people with a newfound dread
As statues are demeaned and hammered down
When black and white create a fearful tension
Which up to now seemed too unclear to mention
As tears and anger sweep 'most every town...

Will the day come when we in our despair
May feel unsure what book we now can dare
Pick from the shelf and read with gusto old?
Will Orwell's vision told in '1984'
Come to fruition soon for evermore
For us to always do what we are told
Or can we still afford to stand up bold
And treasure, please, the freedom that we hold?

13.06.2020

I'm the One Metre Man

I'm the one metre man
Who carries the brush and the can
With the white enamel ready to flow
And erase the '2' when given the go
To ease the restricted proximity
Of how close to each other we now should be…

I'll paint and I'll paint over all the '2's
And turn them to '1' and reduce the queues
Make people get closer in their small huddle
Who knows, perhaps even permit a cuddle?
My brush will be busy, the paint ever flowing
I cannot wait – now let me get going.

All over the country, all over the world
The one metre men, as the virus unfurled,
Were given the task to paint numbers for all
"So close but no nearer, we need to stand tall"
And now as restrictions are starting to bend
Hard workers like me our brushes will lend
To wipe out frustration and give us new hope
How many new '1's – O Lord, can I cope?

But what's this I hear – does somebody say
That '2's down to '1's is not for today?
That we have to find a good compromise
And ready ourselves without thinking twice

To take out the '2's, yes, but here is the laugh
Instead of the '1' paint but one and a half?!

I pick up my bucket in tender despair
And twirl my moustache and ruffle my hair
As undaunted, untouched I resume where I ended
The painting and warning signs being extended
By governments, leaders with much on their mind
Trying so hard for a way out to find...

I am the one metre man
Carrying the brush and the can
Smiling the whole journey through
As I help make life safe for you.

17.06.2020

A Pandemic Glossary in Reverse

See how many pandemic phrases you can find. There are many more I'm sure not listed here – but it's a start. And yes, there's no X – still working on that!

Z   This is sending me to zzzzzzzleeep even before I begin

Y   Years and years to go before we can see an end

W   Working from home becoming the norm as more and more stay in

V   Virus control, vaccine, ventilator – driving us round the bend...

U   'Unprecedented', that word again, as bad as 'amazing' and 'hero'

T   Testing, two metres, or one-and-a-half then down to the beach in a huddle

S   Social distancing, self-quarantining, will it ever get down to zero?

R   Respirator, like headless chicks running, why are we in such a muddle?

Q   Quarantine and questions galore: what can and what cannot be done?

P   Pandemic, pandemonium, PPE – words dwarfing us into fear

O   One metre not two and not even the half restrictions all been and gone

N   New national emergency looming close? Wasn't it always here?

M   Martial law, mortality rates, statistics: some up, some down

L   Lockdown – yes, lockdown, that wonderful word to give us such needed cheer!

K   Keep cool, no surrender, stay safe and stay put, and don't fool around as a clown

J   It's a jungle out there, it's a jumble of laws wearing us down, far from clear...

I   Index case, immune-comprised, incubation and others to boot

H   Herd immunity, hearing, adhering, I'm sorry – it puzzles me so

G   G for gee-wiz, game changer, go get it, the advice can be such a hoot!

F   Flattening the curve or fatality rate, please show me the route to go

E   Epidemic, emerging encounters encroaching from other countries afar

D   D for deficiency, virus sufficiency, testing our painful endurance

C   Covid-19, contract tracing and spreading, I've got you! Oh boy, what a star!

B   B is for beach overflowing and Brexit, for what, what is Brexit, not heard about that for so long?

A   as in apocalypse, Armageddon – and this is the end of my song.

Heaven help us all...

25.06.2020

Processing Problems

Pubs reopened, pints being pulled, all well and good
But not so with processing plants and all manners of food
Where new virus cases emerge almost out of control
Just as we began to believe we might be on a roll

And even some pubs find that almost as soon as they try
The doors have to close with many now wondering why
As light at the end of the tunnel at last seemed to shine
The problems just escalate further and fast down the line

With no end in sight and with many beginning to think
What's wrong with a social time and a wee drop to drink
The virus continues regardless of east and of west
Preparing for lockdown anew as we seek our rest

We're tired, fatigued, on the brink of just waving the flag
In total surrender as obstacles threaten to drag
Us out of our comfort and determination to win
We feel we're so near – then the virus looks on with a grin

It started in China with food being processed all wrong
It continues in Britain the same and we wonder how long
Before we can once again dream our dreams and aspire
To drag ourselves surely but quietly out of the mire?

And 'bubbles' are bubbling as families start getting close
And two metre rulings ignored in favour of those
Who pile to the beaches with barely an inch in between
Pre-empting new outbreaks far worse than we've already
    seen

While plants keep on processing – surely we all need to eat
And pubs try their luck on the road to success, not defeat
But further and further away seems the hope – now a tear
Expressing our doubts, our sadness and above all our fear...

07.07.2020

So Who's Laughing Now Then?

This reflection should be read in conjunction with and following on from 'This is Your Virus Speaking' (p.16).

Well, I'm certainly not. Laughing, I mean. I never envisaged for a moment that I would be that difficult to get rid of, truth be known, and it is draining me to continue to think of new ways of keeping everyone on their toes. When you think about it, not only are they worrying about when I may finally die a sudden death, many are even beginning to think that I may be with them for life, and that they will have to learn to live – or die – with me. And if not with me then with whoever else follows in my wake.

There's a lot of worry about, and not surprisingly when you think about it. And the main reason for the worry is that most people just don't know where they have got me! I mean, when half a million people headed for just one beach on the one very hot day of early summer, half the population thought that this would be the start of the second wave of me. And yet, it seemed to make hardly any difference to anything. And all those protests all over the world against slavery, with millions and millions of people standing within an inch of each other – well, that made hardly any difference to the statistics either.

However, when they opened the pubs and people returned for a welcome drink, just one of my victims could cause the pub to close the next day and all the other punters having to be contacted and in many cases self-isolate. Again. No wonder there's confusion. I'm confused...

And now it appears that most food processing plants are worried sick that they are the prime sources of me spreading out of control, as well they might. Lack of ventilation, they call it, or a sneeze out of place. What do I know? But do I care? Of course I care.

All the while this is happening they continue to try and find a vaccine that will finally get rid of me. Admitting that it could take years, if ever. Acknowledging that I am an adversary unlike any other they have ever come across. What a record that is! And now they are blaming me for the worst recession in living memory and wondering if ever anything anywhere will ever get back to normal.

What do I know? But do I care? Yes, I care. Would I like one day just to quietly implode on myself and stop all this suffering and uncertainty for so many? Yes. But can I see it happening? Not in a hurry, no. Not while everyone is blaming everyone else for what, after all, is nobody's fault, for I am something quite new that no one ever experienced before.

So, who's laughing now then? Are you?

09.07.2020

Is It Now Burka Time for All?

On hearing the news that face covering will be mandatory for all shoppers in England from July 24th and that those refusing could be fined up to £100.

O my word, it's going all to pot!
I used to be quite happy with my lot
But now I wonder where I best might turn
The more confused I am, the more I learn.
You can't do this but must do that for sure
The things that we good folk have to endure
You can't pop to the shop without a scarf
It's getting far too complex now by half.
And as for me, a mask will never do
But just maybe – I wonder about you –
My Liverpool necktie might do the job
Unless you know a better team to swop?
Not many years ago I well remember
How many lands got into quite a temper
About the burka worn in town and city
Thus hiding smiling faces – more the pity –
But now I start to wonder whether next
(and even writing this I feel perplexed)
Not some job's worth in Westminster decree
That burkas will be given out for free
As virus caught within cannot escape
This may just help us into better shape?
And so I rest my case as soon I doubt
I shall see many shoppers walk about…

14.07.2020

And As If All This
Were Not Enough...

We now hear yet again that global warming is a real threat as icebergs break up and threaten to drown us all in no time whatsoever.

It seems to me that wherever we turn we are faced with one disaster after another.

And we may ask ourselves, is life even worth living anymore?

This is where God comes in. Strongly and powerfully. Whether we believe in Him or not. This is where faith becomes our footstool, our hope of salvation.

This is where anything earthly is overshadowed by everything heavenly.

I dare hardly buy a paper or switch on the television these days. but what about that Bible gathering dust on the shelf? Waiting to be opened again after all those years. Dare we? Ought we? Dare we not?

Enough is enough. It's Jesus for me.

16.07.2020

In Tribute to 'A'

While I do not wish to divulge his full or real name, I guess many who read this may know to whom I refer.

Every church coffee morning going, you'd be there
Straight from the off-licence you'd be there
With your daily paper for your cup of coffee
Quietly, unobtrusively sitting there taking in the atmosphere
Enjoying the company of the people coming and going
Though not always entering into conversation with anyone
Still you'd be there, and we loved having you there
Week after week

After a while you even ventured over the threshold to my
    church
Attended the Sunday service
Yes, sometimes you had to leave for a puff and a drink
And you did not always come back
But you were never far away
And one Sunday morning you took Communion – you were
    there

You were there when I had to put up the notices about
    closing church
For as long as it takes
Due to the pandemic
Sitting on the bench by the church
And saying to all who cared to listen
"I so love this place and the people in it"
And you could not wait for us to open
You were there

Then one day the bench was empty
You had been taken into hospital
And you are there now
Terminally ill in high dependency
And I ask myself now that you are there
Do you sense Him with you
The One you came to search for at my church
And I so pray you feel Him there with you...

23.07.2020

Travel (Who Wants It?)

With apologies to those employed in aviation.

Total chaos, no one knowing
Quite which way the wind is blowing
Holidays abroad galore
Who in truth could wish for more?
Except when you get there to roam
No guarantee you will get home

And if you're lucky and return
You can't get back to work and earn
For now you must self-isolate
No wonder many get irate
The hassle just to catch the plane
Suffices to drive one insane

Checks here, forms there, then join the queue
And tempers flare, the air is blue
In strict masked anonymity
We think how travel ought to be
Not all this drabness, that's for sure
Should I go home – wait for a cure?

O Boris, please tell what may be
Of that great bridge across the sea
That you have promised to create
To link all Britain – before too late

Now, can't you build one larger still
If I donate towards the bill?

A worldwide one to countries far
So we can get there in a car!

27.07.2020

Clevedon by the Sea – Here We Come

A pearl of a town with a pier
   and a square for relaxing
For putting aside the things
   of the mind that are taxing
For gently preparing to move
   yet allow the commotion
That also forms part of the turmoil in heart
   and in soul, each emotion...
Enabled, invited to come,
   and yes, once again prove
That few things in life are more challenging
   than when you move.

Preparing to say your farewells
   to the friends that you made
During ten truly wonderful years
   in life's busy arcade
Not to mention the family
   soon to be left, yet still near
Just thirty-five minutes by car,
   no big problem, no fear?
And yet there are times of frustration,
   anxiety too
And no doubt those moments of wondering
   what best to do?

To move is a wrench and a heartbreak
   but also a time for a change

To quietly, peacefully ponder,
    allow the visions and dreams for a range
Of new starts envisaged and wished for
    in a time of pandemic confusion
Yet holding so firmly to the belief
    that God has prepared the solution.

So, Clevedon, we're coming, preparing, uprooting,
    albeit with some looking back
We're praying, consoling, allowing,
    enabling feelings to keep us on track
As time marches on
    and we walk hand in hand
As nearer and nearer
    without any slack
You compel us to dream,
    to look forward and move to a wonderful land.

10.-11.08.2020

When Enough is Enough

Six months of uncertainty, misery, dire ambiguity
Putting our lives on hold in unspeakable ways
Half a year gone with restricted mobility
Making us hermits, controlling our nights and our days
Telling us not when to grasp for hope and a new zest for life
Commanding instead that the fine will be steep for denial
Demanding compliance with every new challenging strife
Adding to burdens already too great in this trial.

Enough is enough
Show us hope, show us love, show us light
And hold the torch high as we follow our Lord on the way
Help us not surrender but in trust and with all our might
Reach the end of the tunnel that leads to a glorious day.

16.08.2020

Is No-one Ever Happy?

A short poem in support of the Government.

Poor exam results. Whom can we blame?
Students in tears, too many to name.
And yet many also got a higher grade
To make their concern, if not vanish, then fade.

Nothing is normal but what can we do
But help one another to see this thing through
And who could do better in times of such strain
To steer a straight course, come sunshine, come rain?

Let those we appointed to govern work on
Until all our fearfulness be conquered and gone
Help us not throw stones but with courage and hope
United in trust show the world how to cope.

20.08.2020

Preparing for a Return to School

The big question now appears to be
Mask or no mask for pupils?
No change there then – for is this not the question we all ask
  ourselves?
And when or where to wear it – or not –
Why not just make it compulsory by default to wear a
  mask? Everywhere.
Not that I enjoy wearing mine
Even if it is a Liverpool Football Club one.
I still hate it.
My beloved hates hers even more
Her glasses steam up so terribly.
Until she heard a newsreader on telly this morning say
That she wears her glasses on top of the mask
And I said to my beloved
'Well, it can't make you look any dafter than you do
  already.'
(I won't be saying that again…)

Children preparing for school
Parents breathing a sigh of relief through their masks
Teachers trying to decide when to wear one themselves
And when to allow the children a respite
For lunch perhaps?
Could be a bit messy otherwise…

Might it just be possible
That the children returning to school
Will propel our society back to some form of normality

Masked – or unmasked –
Or is that too a pie in the sky
In these troubled times?

We might be out of all this in two years' time
Say those in the know but with so little proof
Thank you very much, sir
That's just great, isn't it?
Aren't we all pleased?
Or are we simply trying to mask our displeasure?

To the children of today
So much rides on you
As you prepare for school
And help us prepare to live again.
No pressure...

25.08.2020

First Impressions

We're in
Now the fun can begin
The move executed
But spirits diluted
So much in a mess
Which adds to the stress
The carpets are late
Delays which we hate
No room for our stuff
We've had almost enough…

But then we decide
To go for a ride
Take in the fresh air
Find a bench or a chair
A stroll on the prom
For an hour, then some
Feeling one with creation
And sensing elation

Onto Poet's Walk
For a stroll and a talk
Ending up at the pub
For a drink and some grub
Ere it's time to go home
In the wilderness roam…

"It will be okay"
"We will find a way"
"The garden's been done"

"Soon the mess will be gone"
"But the telly plays up"
"Channel mess up non-stop"
"And our mobiles won't send"
"Perhaps too many a bend?"

Yet the town is a dear
With facilities near
We have all we shall need
Once we get up to speed
Though whatever the task
We must don our mask
Social distance to boot
Oh boy, what a hoot!

The pandemic goes on
Yet one battle is won
We're at home by the sea
My beloved and me!

04.09.2020

Christmas Cancelled?

New restrictions
Expect convictions
Six people at most
Including the host
At any one time
Or be guilty of crime
We wonder each day
Is there ever one way
Of returning to sanity
Without risk to our vanity?
Is anyone sure
Of some way to endure
Now that by numbers we're banned
And even Christmas looks canned
Boxed up in a tin
With no looking in
With all families apart
Without a fresh start
To hopefully make –
How much more can we take?

11.09.2020

Waiting for Church to Reopen

Some already have
But many too soon
Others taking longer to decide
To plan and prepare
Numbers restricted for most
But ironically for church
Which few attend
You are allowed up to thirty
As long as you wear a mask
And don't sing
And sit two metres apart
And don't hold a hymnbook
And forget about the wine for Communion
And help yourself to the bread
Touched by no other human hand
(Or even bring your own)
And follow the one-way system
Is it any wonder many don't bother?
Even among the faithful...

Where is God in all this, we wonder
I wonder
Knowing full well that He is everywhere we are
Or choose not to be
Not to be left out of any situation
But right there in the middle of it
With us and for us
Even if we are not aware
Or choose to ignore Him.

Waiting for church to reopen
But while we wait
Do we fail to acknowledge
That the Head of the Church
Is unconfined
Unrestricted
Uncontrollably everywhere we are
Determinedly wanting to see this through
With us
For us
However long it takes
And at the end
Will welcome us
And say
What were you so worried about?

Waiting for church to reopen?
Better to wait on God as He appears
In the confusion of our minds
In the anxiety of our lives
In our frustration of not knowing
What will happen next
And to whom

Wherever we are, He is
Building or no building
In the freshness of the air
While we walk the promenade
In the beauty of this Indian summer
Holding on firmly
In trust and in confidence

To our hope, our faith
For what else can we do?

19.09.2020

Clevedon Marine Lake 2020 – Solace in a Pandemic

A poem resulting from an invitation by the local free paper to write about the lido – or Marine Lake – in Clevedon.

Newcomers, maybe, my beloved
    and me to the pleasures of Clevedon town
New residents here as with hearts of cheer
    we can treasure the beauty renown
When walking the prom, a quick rest,
    and then some, as we head for Victoria's pier
So grateful indeed for the people we meet
    and the welcome so evident here
But nothing can beat the exceptional treat
    of finding our space by the Lake
To stop in our track with the wall at our back
    and just watch for as long as we take
The swimmers galore there forevermore
    and the joy and the smiles and the hope
At a time of such fear with the virus so near
    sometimes making it harder to cope –
Yet here at the Lake there's the option to make
    all our worries, if not disappear
At least put on hold till the day we are told
    that the day of redemption is near
When again we can smile, walk that precious mile,
    then sit by the Lake and pray

In trust and secure God will help us endure
  as we face each new promising day.

23.09.2020

<u>*Postscript 14.10.2020*</u>
I was not successful – only six poets out of the hundreds who wrote to the committee will have their work published. Am I disappointed? Not a bit.

Total Rubbish

A light-hearted yet serious reflection.

'You won't like it,' she said (long before we even got here)
But North Somerset seems to have more recycling bins and
    various other receptables
Than most other counties in the UK put together
I thought nothing much of it or about it
Until now we've got here
And my beloved was right.

We're still waiting for yet one more container
To add to the six we've already got
As well as the instructions that go with them
Where to put what and why
Or alternatively as the case may be – why not?

I asked my beloved only this morning
Why have such a big black bin next to the green garden one
When to be honest hardly anything is allowed in the big
    black one
But has to go in all the other smaller ones
For recycling, they say?
(I wonder how many and how often someone actually
    checks what is in any of those containers...)

I think of all the trips to the dump in those early days
With all the kind gentlemen
Asking, 'What have you got?'
All packed up in black bags
'Household rubbish,' I'd say

And no one asked for further detail
So in it went – everything – regardless
Into the household rubbish container
Large and bottomless – almost
And you could hear it clunk
Gently but surely as it hit its destination
Except for the cardboard of course
That had to go in the container next door
No big deal

But now the honeymoon is over
And we have no excuse
All the seven containers are here
And lo and behold if Big Brother sees
You putting something in the wrong one!

'You won't like it,' she said
And I don't
But like everyone else I now have to lump it
(and watch how I dump it!)

25.09.2020

And Now, to Trump it All...

The single most powerful man in the world
So often complacent as the virus unfurled
Now landed in hospital with the disease
Though battling on and seeming at ease
Admitting the next day or two will be close
As doctors do checks and administer dose

As into his chopper the President walked
He knew that worldwide people pondered and talked
"Now, will he survive this or is it the end?"
"Will he be more serious or refuse still to bend?"
And will the Election – already a mess –
Lead to further confusion and terrible stress?

This shows that no man or no woman indeed
Can count themselves safe or dampen the speed
Of a virus that travels wherever it knows
That some just don't care however it goes
That we are all targets, in theory at least
Of the Covid-19, a world-shattering beast.

But meanwhile, we hope, and we pray, and we trust
That an end is in sight for we sense that it must
Come to some kind of light at the end of it all
When most people will rise, a minority fall –
So here's to the President, loathe him or like,
That his willpower sends this 19 on its bike!

04.10.2020

A Revolt is Brewing

People have had enough
A simple sniff or a cough
Am I really on death's door?
Feeling a little hot
Yes, maybe, but virus it's not
I have felt this way before.

Hardly daring to think
About seeking the pub for a drink
Lest someone is there with nineteen…
But nor can I stay in the house
As a gentle and meek little mouse
Just waiting for dangers unseen.

Enough is enough, goes the cry
As people are wondering why
The graphs and statistics to scare
Now lay the reality bare
That we cannot and will not lie down
And abolish each city and town.

We can't know how long this will take
Or whether it is make or break
But one thing we all know for sure:
No matter what lies ahead
We must learn to abolish the dread
And summon the strength to endure.

The people say, now is enough
Let's go and take the smooth with the rough

Allow us the gift of Free Will
To face yet another bright day
With God by our side all the way
Seeing us to the top of the hill.

09.-10.10.2020

Christchurch 11.10.20 –
A Reflection

Back in God's house.
Finally.
A building large and imposing but at the same time lovely
  and warm
Numbers restricted
Masks compulsory
Singing banned
Worship band not yet *in situ*
But prayer, a sermon, a couple of worship songs all there…
Good
Loving
An opportunity we have not had for so long…

Communion next Sunday
Cannot remember the last time
Already booked our seats
My beloved and me

Clevedon
Christchurch
You have made us feel welcome
And now the move is complete
Church has reopened
And we were among the first to book
And we shall go
Again and again
Mask or no mask

Until the virus is beaten
And beyond

We need not seek God in church
He is everywhere
Absolutely
And yet
We felt His presence
Encompassing us and everyone there
Welcoming us back
His name be praised...

12.10.2020

Shutdown Wales?

Another two weeks of rejection and misery?
Without access or escape?
Another total meltdown in free movement
And restricted communication
With no chance to meet
As family or friend
Across the border

And will it work?
Is this the way to kill the virus?
Has it not been tried before?
And did it make any difference then?

Does anything make any difference any longer?
Does anyone know what to do for the best
Without fearing the worst?
Is the nightmare coming to an end
Or just beginning?

Does anyone care much any longer?
Do I?
Does God?
Yes, God does.
The bread and the wine reminded us on Sunday
That this is his promise
And means to salvation
Amidst the adversity
In lingering doubt
And exaggerated fear
That He is there, that He is here

In Wales as in Somerset
Lending a hand
Forcing a smile
Wiping a tear
Hope against hope
Love everlasting
Saying to all with ears to hear
That things will get better...

Shutdown Wales?
Soon we shall know.
Shutdown God?
Not now, not ever.

19.10.2020

Please, Sir, When May We Demask?

I'm tiring of wearing a mask
To fulfil so many a task
And fed up with having to hide
My features in which I take pride
The face without which I am nil
All covered – so bitter a pill –
When having too much to rely
On what we can see with the eye.

Our breathing is troublesome too
And the wearing of glasses taboo
As they steam and make vision so dire
This pandemic has gone to the wire
And people are getting frustrated
Now the do's and the don't's have abated
And the mind is now focused instead
On when to uncover your head!

So, Boris, this is guaranteed
To regain your power at speed:
Permit us our common sense
To release that within us so tense
To view once again this sad world
As it was when the virus unfurled
Not perfect, far from it in fact
Yet allowing our lives stay intact.

For now it is getting beyond
We no longer know how to respond
To dangers both unknown and tall

Where once we would stand, now we fall
Begin with that mask-covered face
And may this see the end of the race
For no one will ever endure
A mask where we cannot be sure
How much it protects and prevents
Compared to the oxygen tents!

26.-27.10.2020

Second National Lockdown

Another month of "Don't do this and must do that"
Of restricted movement and social engagement
Of rules and regulations too numerous to list
Not to mention, understand
Of staying put at home
Yet exercising outside as much as you like
Of speaking to your neighbour over the garden fence
But only one at a time, not two
Of keeping inside a sacred space
With you and your God
And no other human allowed
Family or friend
Of forgetting all about God's free will
The greatest gift He ever gave us
Forgetting almost what that gift suggests...

Not doing what is best for me
But ask what would Jesus do in my situation?
For others not as fortunate
Not expecting to be the healer of all ills
But being allowed to make mistakes
Learning from experiences
Putting God first
Yet knowing we often forget
That God still loves us regardless

Second lockdown of a complete country
Yet schools remain open
Children are let loose

Young people too
Students in colleges and universities
Objecting to their restrictions
Yet 'freer' than most

In Denmark, mass killings of mink
To avoid yet another strand of the pandemic
Will this work?
Or will other animals have to be culled too
Down the line?
Is anyone safe?
Are we still allowed our Free Will
To live or to die
Or try and exist somewhere in between the two?
And then this morning
On my TV
The Archbishop of Canterbury
Talking at length about Jesus
And about the need for churches
To be allowed to reopen
Reversing the curfew...?

Unlikely to happen, I know
Still light in the darkness
Just being able to talk about it
Pray about it, think about it
To talk about Jesus
An open door when all else seems shut...

05. 06.11.2020

A Light at the End of the Tunnel – Perhaps?

At long last the news that a vaccine may be near
To give us light in all the gloom, alleviate our fear
And that perhaps in a few weeks it may be set to go
And reach the frontline people first who frankly need it so
And then the rest of us, no doubt, but further down the line
I must be patient and not rush to put a stamp on mine
For there are many more deserving, this I truly know
But may this be the start of something good, and may it
   grow!

09.11.2020

Decidedly Lowkey

Despite the better news no great sense of euphoria
Yet
It's as if we want so much to hope and pray and trust
Yet hesitate to dare
As if there are still so many unknowns to combat
Before again we dare feel free.

The scaremongers among us
Some scientists not least
Are having a field day
With gloomy statistics quenching the light
The brightness of a new day which
For just one moment
We were encouraged and allowed to believe in.

The media – the papers
Hope and glory on one page
Devastation on the next
New keywords appearing
Like rolling out
Vaccines, not just the one
But several all at once
About to be rolled out
But will they all work
Will any – completely –
And if they do, how?
And for whom?
For how long?

We feel decidedly low-key
Where in so many ways we should be feeling on a high
As we continue to hope against hope
Trust in the face of the facts
Pray in the silence of our hearts and minds
To our Lord who we know is listening
But whose answers we cannot
Or will not
Always hear

But low-key
Is better than no key
To unlock the door
To a new beginning
Surely?

12.11.2020

Dorothy

How uplifting it is even in, or perhaps especially thanks to, these extraordinary times for Margaret and me to feel guided and inspired to commit her Mum's poems and reflections over so many years to our laptops before the handwritten pages fade never to be recovered. Dorothy, born in 1911, lived to be almost a hundred years old and by the looks of things began seriously writing in her mid-twenties, and our work of restoration is truly a labour of love with no real end in sight – but that does not matter. Here's to Dorothy in memoriam and with love from us both.

At a time of such extreme confusions
Hope and fear yet mixed with resolutions
How – when this is over – we might change
The two of us are spending precious time
Delving into Dorothy's mighty rhyme
As in her writing she comes so alive
Expressing the love of God she'd always strive
To share with those who came to love her best
Pointing to Him yet leave to Christ the rest.

No pressure ever, no precise dictate
For Mum so knew that some would see Him late
But always words of courage, love and hope
To show how in distress we may still cope
And so the work of love we now both share
Helps us divert our eyes from much despair.

Mum never lost her faith in her good Lord
She'd give Him all the time she could afford
From early years with work and family ties
She penned her words and sent to God her cries

Of questions many, yes, but such assurance
Which we now treasure in our joint endurance.

We see right here in doing what we do
In 1919 came right out of the blue
A virus not dissimilar to now...
Not long after a baby girl was born
In growing up she might have felt forlorn
But soon in God's own light she took a bow.

She never stopped her quest to know Him better
And found her way to make Him real by letter
In writings that before they fade away
We now commit to laptop day by day
In praise and love for one to us so dear
Who helps us sense our Saviour ever near.

No worldly curse will ever kill the light
That He extends to all by His sheer might
And so we ask as now we labour on
Like Dorothy, one day, our work be done...

17.-18.11.2020

Christmas On Hold?

Can we? Should we? Ought we stay behind
And other ways to celebrate the season find?
Ask ourselves what really Christmas is about
Beyond the turkey and the brussels sprout!
Beyond the need, the right we feel to see
All our beloved (wherever they may be)
'Let's travel,' goes the cry. 'Let's join together
Regardless of the risk, inclement weather
And public transport trying to reduce
The service offered – I am no recluse –
It is my privilege to take these days
And worry later who exactly pays
For increased tension, virus victims as with glee
I just sit back and say, "It won't be me."'

It is not over, still some way to go
Despite the vaccine that we longed for so
About to be available, we trust
Before we see economies go bust

Now is the time for patience to the fore
Lest we succumb to Covid evermore
And find the reason to comply in love
And trust ourselves to His deep grace above
Who holds us in His arms and helps us see
We're in His care wherever we may be

And so, the two of us will simply stay
And trust in Him to help each see a way
Out of the mire to joys, as yet unfound,

Where opportunities will soon abound
A Happy Christmas is our fervent hope
In seeking His good strength to help us cope.

26.11.2020

Good News Galore

Good news galore to bring to the fore
First vaccine arrived for which many strived
And tested and toiled yet with questions embroiled:
'Can this really be true for me and for you
That we're on our way to the light of the day?
Will it work and evolve to now finally solve
The fear and the doubt and again make us shout
Hallelujah indeed, from the virus we're freed
Or is it all a bit soon to go into a swoon?'

In the US indeed they question the speed
With which in this land we can now make a stand
And in other world parts they have made different starts
That may or may not seem to brighten our dream...

More vaccines to come, at least three and then some
Successful in tests but who will know best
Which to use and for whom in this age steeped in gloom?

We're right to rejoice yet consider the voice
Urging caution in joy lest we go and destroy
The signs that we see, what again may soon be
Round the corner for all when the virus does fall.

For the end is in sight sure as day follows night
Yet with some time to wait for the opening gate
Letting in once again the cure for our pain
As we travel along, dancing, singing our song.

04.12.2020

Similar Books from the Publisher

Selah by Linda Daruvala
ISBN 978-1-78815-610-3

'Selah' is a Hebrew word that appears in many of the biblical psalms, instructing the listener to pause and reflect on what has just been sung. This spiritually nourishing collection of poems was written as Linda Daruvala paused and reflected on Christian retreats and in places of stillness. From poetic paintings of God's creation to a Psalm-like outpouring of her heart to God, Linda echoes the experiences and emotions that are common to many of us in our journey with the Lord.

Raised from Dust by Alison Stedman
ISBN 978-1-911086-82-6

In this collection of poems, Alison takes us on a journey around the world, from the familiar sight of a homeless man on the streets to the wonders of Asian countryside and culture. With sentiments echoing Ecclesiastes, she mourns the transient nature of our lives and all that we see around us. She then flips the coin and explores birth and rebirth, leading to a hope that transcends our temporal existence here on earth.

Available from all good bookshops or from the publisher:
www.onwardsandupwards.org